BOOK REPAIR AND RESTORATION

A MANUAL OF PRACTICAL SUGGESTIONS
FOR BIBLIOPHILES

Including some Translated Selections

from

Essai sur l'art de Restaurer les Estampes et les Livres,
par A. Bonnardot, Paris 1858

By

MITCHELL S. BUCK

Author of "Syrinx," "Ephemera," "The Songs of Phryne,"
Translator of "Lucian's Dialogues of the Hetaerai," etc.

Philadelphia   NICHOLAS L. BROWN   MCMXVIII

COPYRIGHT, 1918
BY NICHOLAS L. BROWN

Printed July 1918

This scarce antiquarian book is included in our special *Legacy Reprint Series*. In the interest of creating a more extensive selection of rare historical book reprints, we have chosen to reproduce this title even though it may possibly have occasional imperfections such as missing and blurred pages, missing text, poor pictures, markings, dark backgrounds and other reproduction issues beyond our control. Because this work is culturally important, we have made it available as a part of our commitment to protecting, preserving and promoting the world's literature. Thank you for your understanding.

INLAID LEVANT BINDING
(Frontispiece)

FOREWORD

The following chapters contain suggestions partly gathered from the experience of others and partly evolved for myself in caring for my own books. Although many "books about books" have already been written, there is still, I think, a place for this one. I have designed it especially for the bibliophile who enjoys "fussing" over his books and who receives, in seeing them in good condition and repair through his own efforts, an echo of the pleasure he receives from reading them.

In translating from Bonnardot, I have taken the liberty of abridging or paraphrasing, at times, the chapters which I have included here, not only to confine the subjects a little more closely but also to present his essential suggestions as concisely as possible. His book, copies of which are very scarce, was first issued in an edition of four hundred copies in 1846 and re-issued, with revisions, in 1858. It has not since been reprinted nor, so far as I have been able to learn, has it been translated into English, either wholly or in part.

CONTENTS

FOREWORD: Page 7

Chapter I
GENERAL RESTORATION: Page 15

Chapter II
REMOVING STAINS: Page 25

Chapter III
REBACKING: Page 39

Chapter IV
REPAIRING OLD BINDING: Page 51

Chapter V
REBINDING: Page 77

Chapter VI
THE BOOK SHELVES: Page 89

Chapter VII
BOOK BUYING: Page 99

Chapter VIII
THE GREEK AND LATIN CLASSICS: Page 111

INDEX: Page 123

LIST OF ILLUSTRATIONS

INLAID LEVANT BINDING: *Frontispiece*
RE-LINING BACK: Page 21
VELLUM BINDINGS: Page 25
ORIGINAL SHEEP BINDING (1684) REBACKED: Page 39
CUTTING FOR REBACKING: Page 41
CUTTING FOR REBACKING: Page 42
LOOSENING LEATHER FOR REBACKING: Page 43
SETTING NEW BACK: Page 44
BINDING HEAD-CAP: Page 45
FOLDER: Page 47
IRON: Page 48
MODERN LEVANT BINDING: Page 51
SOLANDER SLIP-CASE: Page 77
LEATHER SLIP-COVERS: Page 89
SLIP-COVER: Page 92
KELMSCOTT PRESS BOOK: Page 99
BLACK LETTER VIRGIL: Page 111

CHAPTER I
GENERAL RESTORATION

To consider first a few simple processes of ordinary restoration, let us assume that a rare book in its original cloth or boards, in a more or less damaged condition but not to the point of necessitating rebinding, has just been received.

The first operation required is to carefully clean off the binding with a soft cloth, wipe off the end papers, which often have a coating of dust, especially when the covers do not fit closely, and, if the top is gilt, wipe that carefully also. An "uncut" top is freed from dust by brushing with a soft brush.

The book is then collated to make sure that every page is in place and, if there are plates, that no plate is missing. This operation, it is perhaps needless to say, should by all means be done before purchasing, unless the book comes from a reliable dealer to whom an imperfect copy could be returned. If, in collating an old book, the amateur discovers that page 173 follows immediately after page 136, he need not necessarily be alarmed, as mistakes in pagination and even in the numbering of signatures are very common in books printed a century or more ago. In such cases, the "catch words" which generally appear at the bottom of the pages, or else the text itself, should be examined to see whether the page, without regard for its number, is really in its proper place or not. Each page is then examined for dirt or finger marks, which can almost always be removed, the quality of the paper permitting, with a soft pencil-eraser or bread crumbs.

Marginal notes, especially in contemporary hands, are much better left alone; they are often of considerable value and, when neatly and not excessively done, rather add to the interest of the volume without detracting from its value to any great extent. On which subject Bonnardot has quite a little to say, in the chapter on *Stains* included in this volume.

Presentation inscriptions in the autograph of the author or of some one intimately connected with him of course greatly increase the interest and value of the book. Names written on title-pages can often be effaced by the process elsewhere described, but these should not be disturbed until they have been thoroughly investigated. A name which at the moment seems totally unfamiliar may sometimes be found of special interest inscribed in the particular volume in which it is found. As an ordinary illustration of this, might be mentioned a copy of Edwin

Arnold's "Gulistan" bearing on the half-title the inscription "To dear Mrs. Stone from Tama." This author had, at one time, married a Japanese girl, and a little investigation revealed that her name was Tama KuroKawa. Her inscription, of course, remains undisturbed, as it adds a distinctly personal note to the volume. But alas! the John Diddles and William Bubbles who have for centuries scribbled their odious names over fair title-pages, with never the grace to make themselves immortal and their autographs a find!

Writing in the year 1345, Richard de Bury remarks, "When defects are found in books, they should be repaired at once. Nothing develops more rapidly than a tear, and one which is neglected at the moment must later be repaired with usury." Bearing in mind these words of wisdom while examining each page of the book, pencil notes should be made on a slip of paper of any pages needing repairs, also of any places between the signatures where the back is "shaken" exposing the stitching and lining.

Checking off from this list, advisable repairs should then be made. The edges of any tears should be neatly joined with paste. To do this, a clean sheet of white paper should be placed under the torn part and the edges of the tear lightly coated with ordinary white paste. These edges are then pressed together by means of another sheet of white paper pressed above, both the upper and under sheets being gently moved several times to prevent them from sticking to the torn edges. Paste used in this way dries in a few minutes and holds firmly if the edges of the tear are a bit rough. If the page is separated by a clean cut, it may be necessary to apply a strip of thin tissue to hold the edges together. The same general method may be used for inlaying pieces torn from the margins, perhaps by the careless use of a paper cutter in the hands of the original owner. Paper of the same weight and tint as the torn page is secured, placed under the lacuna, and the outlines of the missing part traced off with a sharp pencil. The piece to be inlaid is then cut, following the traced outline but leaving a little margin, and pasted in position, the outer edge being cut even with the general edge of the leaf when the inlay is dry. (*)

White paper for inlaying may be tinted with watercolors to match the old paper. The best method, however, of imitating the yellowish tone of old paper is to stain the inlay with potassium permanganate. This is a dark purple crystal which is used in extremely weak solution in warm

(*) M. R. Yve-Plessis in his "Petit Essai de Biblio-Therapeutique" suggests an excellent way of preparing a paper patch for an inlay. Which is, to lay the paper from which the patch is to be taken under the torn page and trace the outlines of the tear on the new paper with a clean pen filled with water. By tracing over several times, the water will saturate the new paper on the line made by the pen, so that the paper may be pulled apart, providing a patch having more exact outlines than could be secured by cutting with scissors.

water. If a sheet of paper is to be tinted for inlaying or to replace, perhaps, a missing fly-leaf, it is laid in the solution for a few seconds, then removed and the excess purple tone thoroughly washed off under running water. The paper will then be found tinted a pale, yellowish brown, the tone of which may be varied by the strength of the solution and the length of time the paper remains in it. Coffee, licorice or tobacco may also be used, with good results.

The pages all in order and repair, the next operation is to repair the "shaken" back. Perhaps there is no ill to which old books, especially modern issues in their original bindings, are more subject. The damage known as "broken" back usually means a book practically broken in half, the break, in old calf bindings, usually extending through to the outside of the back. The "shaken" back on the contrary, has merely separated between the signatures, exposing, between the inside sheets, the lining of the back. Cheaply bound books seldom remain solid between the signatures, especially when they are printed on heavy, unyielding paper. The damage arises partly from the drying out of the glue in the back and partly from careless handling by readers. Books should always be opened gently and never forced open to absolutely flatten out the pages unless the binding is known to be entirely safe and firm.

The breaks between signatures are repaired and the old glue at these points softened by means of bookbinders' paste. For this, a solid, satisfactory and fairly elastic substitute can be made by mixing about equal parts of good liquid glue and ordinary white library paste of the kind which comes in tubes. With a long pin, slightly bent on the point, this mixture is laid in the open crack between the signatures, care being taken to distribute it evenly the whole length of the book and to thoroughly cover the exposed inside of the back lining. An excess of paste must be avoided, as it would spread out on the inside margins of the leaves when the book is closed to dry. When all the broken places are mended, the book is closed and placed under a slight pressure for a few hours.

Where the book is bound with a "spring back," that is to say, with a back which springs apart when the book is opened, leaving a space between the outside back and the actual back of the signatures where they are stitched, a further strengthening of the back may be desirable. This strengthening can be obtained by "lining up" the inside back with a new strip of paper.

To do this, cut a strip of medium weight Japan vellum—which is the best paper for the purpose—a few inches more than twice the height of the book and in width equal to the inside back. One end of this, with the corners clipped so it will not catch, is inserted between the outside and inside backs of the book and slipped through until it projects about an inch at the bottom of the book. (Fig. A.) The part of the strip left exposed at the top is then well coated on the inside face with the paste mentioned above and pulled into the book, against the inside back or lining, by means of the end projecting at the bottom. The surplus of the strip at top and bottom is

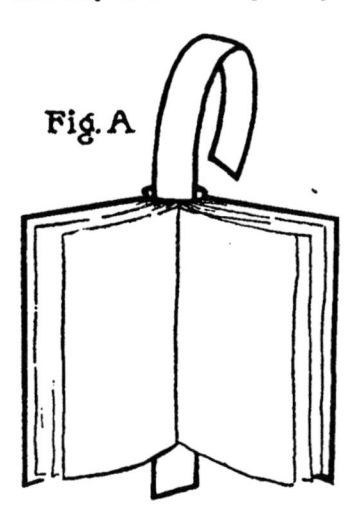

Fig. A

then cut off, two short slips of paper temporarily inserted at top and bottom to prevent the new lining adhering to the outside back, and a firm hand pressure applied all over the back to force the new lining into close union with the old on the backs of the signatures. The book is then set aside to dry, under a light pressure, after which the two slips of paper inserted at top and bottom are pulled out.

Any slight necessary exterior repairs should then be made—loose bits of cloth or paper at worn corners or along the edges of the boards pasted down, and any tears at the top of back above the head-band reenforced from the inside with strips of cloth or paper.

The outside of a soiled cloth binding often may be cleaned by means of a soft pencil-eraser. If this is done, the cloth should afterward be freshened by a thin coat of sizing.

If these operations are carefully and thoroughly carried out, the book should then be in a solid and satisfactory condition and capable of standing any reasonable amount of wear.

CHAPTER II
REMOVING STAINS
Translated From Bonnardot

VELLUM BINDINGS
(1674 AND 1878)

Before discussing the means of attacking stains which may blemish a book or a precious print, I am going to say that, in certain cases, it might be very desirable to allow them to remain. If I possessed, for example, a missive addressed to Charles IX during the night of Saint Bartholomew, and stained with bloody finger-prints, I would take great care not to disturb these marks which, supposing their authenticity established, would increase tenfold the value of the autograph. If the custodian of the Laurentian Library at Florence should efface, from his Longus manuscript, Paul Louis Courier's puddle of ink, he would commit an act of vandalism, for that ink stain is a literary celebrity. (*)

(*) In 1809 Paul Louis Courier discovered at Florence a complete manuscript of Daphnis and Chloe, containing a long passage in Part I which was missing in all texts known until that time, and the existence of which, as a connecting passage, had long been a subject of speculation among scholars. Unfortunately, he had hardly more than completed a transcript of his discovery when he accidentally upset a bottle of ink over the

To speak of more ordinary examples: one often finds on a book or print, a signature or inscription which may sometimes be an autograph well worth preservation. (*) I very rarely efface signatures or the notes of early, unknown owners; I find it pleasanter to respect these souvenirs of the past. In the same way, some curious objects have certain defects which, I think, add to their interest. For example, a statuette of the Virgin, in silver or ivory, of which the features and hands are half effaced by the frequent contact of pious lips. Restore such worn parts, and the sentiment is stripped from a relic of past ages. It is far better to leave untouched such scars, which attest the antique piety of the cloister. A vellum Book of Hours of the Fifteenth Century, worn and soiled through prayer, has, to my mind, acquired a venerable patina. Here, a spot of yellow wax; there, the head of a saint blemished

original manuscript, partly obliterating the passage. The incident caused a bitter controversy among scholars. Courier was violently attacked and, although he had fifty copies of his text printed for special distribution, was even accused of purposely spilling the ink in order to render his transcript unique.

M. S. B.

(*) M. R. Yve-Plessis, elsewhere quoted, suggests that it may sometimes be desirable to strengthen the ink of some valuable and desirable signature, instead of removing it, and for this purpose recommends a mixture of: Tannin, six grammes; alcohol, thirty-five grammes; distilled water, one hundred grammes; applied with a small brush and the part afterwards brushed over several times with clear water. This operation, however, should certainly not be undertaken except in extreme cases where the signature appeared ready to entirely fade out.

M. S. B.

by the star-print from a tear of devotion: are not these stains which should be respected? On the other hand, a blot of ink or an oily smear point only to carelessness and should be removed.

About the year 1846, I was invited by M. A. Farrens, a skilful restorer of old books, to see in his work-shop a Dance Macabre in quarto, imprinted on paper, at Paris, toward the end of the Fifteenth Century; a rare volume which he was restoring for M. Techner.

The portions already cleaned and restored, compared with those still untouched, excited my admiration. The numerous worm holes, the torn places, had disappeared through an application of paper-paste, so well joined, so well blended in the mass, that I could hardly detect the boundaries of the restorations. The letters and wood-cuts suffering from lacunae had been reformed with great skill on a new foundation. The soiled surfaces of the pages had entirely disappeared before I know not what scraping or chemical action. In a word, M. Farrens was putting into use every secret of restoration to give again to this volume its original lustre.

Ah well! today, I confess, that if I possessed this book in the dilapidated state in which I saw it, I would leave it just as it stood, and limit myself to the indispensable repair of a new and solid binding. Its worn and soiled condition came, very probably, from the frequent and pious turning of its pages, in that monachal perseverance of prayer of which our century knows nothing. Its shocking and decrepit condition had, to my eyes, a secret in harmony with all books of the kind, which, from each page, recall to us our insignificance.

No doubt many amateurs will not agree with me in this; some, perhaps, will declare I have arrived at a monstrous degree of cynicism for a bibliophile. However, I will supply the means of restoring at least a part of their original freshness to books and old prints badly treated by time or by the indifference of their earlier possessors.

When a print is soiled with spots or foreign color, especially in the most interesting places, one can hardly lay it away in a portfolio without making some attempt to remove or reduce the strange tints which appear on it. This is the part of my present work most difficult to discuss, while being the most useful. My simple notions of chemistry are not always sufficient and perhaps, some day, some chemist especially trained in analysis and decomposition may, with advantage, rewrite this portion of my work. I will at least record, however, a large number of satisfactory results which I have obtained and even repeated on fragments of proofs on unsized paper, this last being the most unfavorable of all conditions. (*)

(*) In a note on this subject, Bonnardot warns the amateur against careless or unskilful use of the various chemicals mentioned, as many of them, improperly handled, not only irreparably damage the page or print, but also inflict serious injury on the operator himself.   M. S. B.

The first difficulty comes when the nature of the spot is not easily recognized. This yellow spot which resists both washing and bleaching, may perhaps be formed by some greasy body or by some metallic oxide, and one must proceed carefully on any hypothesis which may be formed. In such cases, where experiments must be tried, it is necessary to know some chemical substance which can be first applied, to the end that, if the spot persists, the chemicals used in attempting its removal will not, at least, render it impervious to further efforts. It is not possible to set positive rules for this. I have tried indifferently the action of an acid before that of an alkali, and vice versa. Only, I have been careful, before renewing any experiments to soak the print for several hours in cold water to stop the action of any chemicals already used and to annul their traces and effects.

The first attempt to make upon a spot of unknown origin, is to soak the print for several hours in cold water and then rub the spot gently with a finger or a small brush. It sometimes happens, especially when the paper has been well made and well sized, that the spot will yield to this gentle rubbing, slide off and disappear. When the spot becomes thick and pasty, it is at least weakened even if it does not come off. This is, in any case, a necessary first operation. But is should be carried out with care, in order not to injure the surface of the print. Before soaking a print in water or chemicals, it is best to clip a few small shreds from the margin and soak these in a small glass test-tube to note the effect. (*)

It sometimes happens that there appears on a page or print a single spot which it is desirable to remove without going to the trouble and risk of soaking the whole sheet. A spot on the corner offers few obstacles; the part is simply dipped in a vessel containing the proper solution. If the spot is in the middle of the sheet, I usually make use of a shallow porcelain cup having sides slanted in toward the centre, such as is used for water-colors. By means of such a cup, any part of a sheet can be brought into contact with the solution. The chemical may also be applied directly to the spot by means of a small brush.

M. de Fontelle advises the use of blotting paper from which a hole, a little larger than the spot, has been cut. This is placed over the spot and the chemical liquid dropped in. The blotter around the spot will absorb the excess liquid without offering any obstacle to the operation.

In operations upon single spots, the action of the chemicals always extends a little beyond the spot itself and often leaves a bleached line which is in disagreeable

(*) After sheets have been cleaned by soaking or washing, they should be re-sized. Sizing is made by dissolving half an ounce of isinglass in a pint of water. The mixture is used at a temperature of about one hundred and twenty-five degrees Fahrenheit and in a shallow pan. Sheets are left in for a few seconds only and then dried between sheets of blotting paper. Sizing will often restore old paper which has become soft.   M. S. B.

contrast with the other parts of the sheet. This may be retinted with dark licorice or some suitable color in more or less concentrated solution, mixed sometimes with a little common ink. This is applied with a small brush, care being taken not to overlap the solution on the unbleached portion of the sheet beyond the bleached line. (*)

REMOVING STAINS OF VARIOUS KINDS

GREASE. Grease spots, especially when very recent, can sometimes be drawn out by an absorbent powder such as impalpable clay or chalk. The spotted leaf is enclosed between two tins or boards, both sides of the spot well dusted with the powder, and the book closed tightly and set aside for several hours. Some kinds of grease absorb more slowly than others. If this operation is unsuccessful, alcohol, ether or benzine may be tried. (†) A weak solution of pure or caustic potash operates very rapidly.

(*) Potassium permanganate, described in the chapter on *General Restoration*, is applicable for this operation. In operating on a spot on the page of a bound book, care should be taken always to place two or three sheets of clean blotting paper under the page to prevent any liquid from soaking through to the next page. M. S. B.

(†) Applied with a brush, first around the outside of the spot, then in narrowing circles until the centre is reached. Blotting paper is then placed on both sides of the sheet, over the spot, and a hot flat-iron applied. The absorbent powder ("French Chalk" answers very well) will operate better if the powdered sheet is enclosed simply between two pieces of paper, and a hot flat-iron applied. Plenty of powder should be used.
M. S. B.

If the ink on the page or print is turned gray by this, it may be restored by a wash of acid in very weak solution.

WHITE OF YELLOW WAX. These spots yield promptly to pure turpentine, especially in a warm bath. When the spots thicken, they are lifted off with a scraper, or blotting paper may be applied, pressed down with a heated iron.

STEARINE. Wax tapers are today replaced by a kind of liquid grease, stearine, spots of which give paper a disagreeable transparency. These dissolve in warm alcohol or boiling water, but the spot remains stiff and the brilliance of the ink is reduced. The greater part of the stearine spot may be removed by the same process indicated for wax.

SEALING WAX. RESIN AND RESINOUS VARNISH. All dry resins yield to a warm alcohol bath. The thick part is removed as above. Sealing wax colored red, blue, etc., leaves a corresponding tint which is very tenacious.

TAR, PITCH, etc. These spots are rarely encountered. They give way to warm turpentine or cold benzine. If a dark trace remains, it sometimes may be removed by oxalic acid if the spot has not been burned by the hot tar. Whenever turpentine is used on any spots, it should always be the purest obtainable.

EGG YELLOW. This is always mixed with a little albumen, a matter which thickens in boiling water and can be drawn from the paper, along with the yellow. If the paper is smooth and well sized, all will disappear under a sponge in a bath of hot water. There sometimes remains a yellowish trace. To remove this, apply with a brush chlorated lime and then very weak hydrochloric acid.

MUD. This may be removed simply with a wet sponge or in a warm water bath. Where the paper is rough and absorbent, soap jelly should be used. If a dark trace remains, it usually will yield to oxalic acid or cream of tartar.

INK. Ordinary writing ink is easily decomposed because its principal constituent is a vegetable matter, oak-gall, mixed with a little iron oxide. This gives way rather promptly to an application or sorrel salt dissolved in boiling water. The water must be boiling to secure prompt action. Even better success may be obtained by the use of pure oxalic acid, which is an extraction from sorrel salt of which it is the base. (*) Chinese ink cannot be

(*) Before and after using oxalic acid on ink stains, it is best to wash the spot or page with hydrochloric acid mixed with about seven times its volume of water. In bleaching ink from a page, a white mark almost always remains, especially noticeable if the paper is tinted with age. It is far better to soak the whole page, to secure uniform bleaching, and then, if necessary, retint the page to its former color, than to attempt to operate on part of a page only. Sometimes, when a book is loosely bound, the page can be carefully cut out, close to the

dissolved but sometimes may be washed from a smooth page by means of a damp sponge. Marking ink may be removed with chloride of lime.

FRUIT JUICE. Stains from fruit may be removed by chlorine or cream of tartar. In some cases, water alone is sufficient.

BLOOD. These stains may be bleached by chloride of lime. As this must be applied for at least twenty minutes, it is better to use it as a damp paste. There will remain a yellow trace which will give way to a weak acid.

FECAL MATTERS OR URINE. For such spots, try soap and water. If this is unsuccessful try successively chlorine, alkalis, oxalic acid and hydrochloric acid, soaking the page for an hour in water between each operation.

TRANSFERRED IMPRESSIONS. Frequently the characters of a book, bound before the ink is completely dry, offset, while in press, an impression in grayish tones upon the opposite pages or upon the faces of inserted prints. These transferred impressions may sometimes be removed by rubbing with an eraser made of bread crumbs or by

sewing, and pasted in again when it has been washed and dried as desired. This is, however, a questionable practice, and may seriously injure the value of the book, and on a valuable book it is better to cut the sewing and remove the entire signature, then have the book rebound, or resewn and returned to the old covers, as may be most advisable.   M. S. B.

soap-jelly, which should be left on for some time and then washed off.

I have no doubt neglected to describe more than one kind of spot which an amateur may find. By analogous reasoning, however, he may find for himself the proper remedies to use. If the spot seems to be of a vegetable or animal nature, he should use chlorine and sulfuric acid; if metallic, diluted hydrochloric acid; if oily or greasy, essence of turpentine, ether, alkaline solutions or benzine.

BLEACHING. (*) Soaking a print in cold water for about twenty-four hours often suffices to brighten and clear it; but if, after a long soaking, it still remains darkened to the point of detracting from the clarity of the engraving, one will need to use chemicals in order to obtain a suitable bleaching. Chloride of lime may be used for this purpose. This is a fine, dry powder which softens when allowed to absorb moisture from the atmosphere. About fifty grammes of this are placed in a bottle about two-thirds full of water, and thoroughly shaken. When the solution clears by the excess of matter

(*) Bonnardot mentions several processes for bleaching a print, equally applicable to the same operation on the pages of a book. I translate the process which seems to be the simplest and most effective. It will be noted that he does not mention the size of the bottle in which the amount of chemical he advises is to be dissolved. I would suggest a full quart bottle, and also that the amateur operator thoroughly try the effect of his solution on some old pieces of paper to make sure it is too weak to injure the body of the paper. M. S. B.

depositing on the bottom of the bottle, the clear liquid is carefully poured off. Another solution, which will be weaker, may be made by pouring more water into the bottle. The clear solution is diluted with about twenty times its quantity of pure water, for use. It is better to dilute too much, and add more of the solution later, if necessary, than to dilute too little. The solution will not injure the black ink of an impression, but if too concentrated, it will make the paper brittle.

After using this solution, the print should be placed in a bath of weak acid, and then left to soak for several hours in clear water.

CHAPTER III
REBACKING

ORIGINAL SHEEP BINDING
(1684 REBACKED)

It often happens that books are purchased in old sheep, calf, or even morocco bindings with the hinges so broken that the boards are either entirely off or held only by weakened cords. Such books may be properly entrusted to a good binder for rebinding in substantial leather. It is sometimes preferable, however, merely to reback such books, not only in order to preserve the old leather sides, which are generally in much better condition than the back and often possessed of a very attractive patina, but also to save the wear and slight trimming to which the book would necessarily be subject in rebinding.

It is inadvisable to reback with calf or any very perishable leather. A good quality morocco should be used. In rebacking books bound in old calf or sheep, a smooth-grain brown morocco, such as that known to the trade as Spanish morocco, will be found satisfactory and a fair match for the old leather, both in color and surface texture.

The first operation in rebacking is to treat the old leather with a softening substance, such as vaseline, to prevent the old leather from breaking while it is being worked on. The vaseline should be rubbed well into the covers, left on for about half an hour, and the excess then wiped off with a soft cloth.

Vaseline is also used in the same way to assist in the preservation of old leather bindings still in good repair. It is not entirely satisfactory, as it soon dries out. The best composition for preserving leather is one suggested by Mr. Douglas Cockerell, made by mixing about two ounces of castor oil with one ounce of paraffin wax. The oil is heated and the wax, shredded, melted into it. As the mixture cools it is stirred with a splinter of wood. If this is thoroughly done, the resulting mixture will be a whitish jelly. A thin coat of this is applied to the leather, especially around the hinges, and well rubbed in with the palm of the hand. Any excess is then wiped off and the book polished with a very soft white rag. This mixture is best used while still hot, a little being soaked into a woolen cloth, by means of which it is rubbed on the binding. If leather bindings could be given this treatment about once a year their life would be greatly increased.

After the leather of the old book to be rebacked has been treated, a cut is made down each side of the back, through the leather close to the broken hinge. (Fig. A.) Care should be taken not to cut through the cords which are set into the boards at this point. If the back is furnished with a leather label in a fair state of preservation, this label should be cut around and lifted off to be used again on the new back.

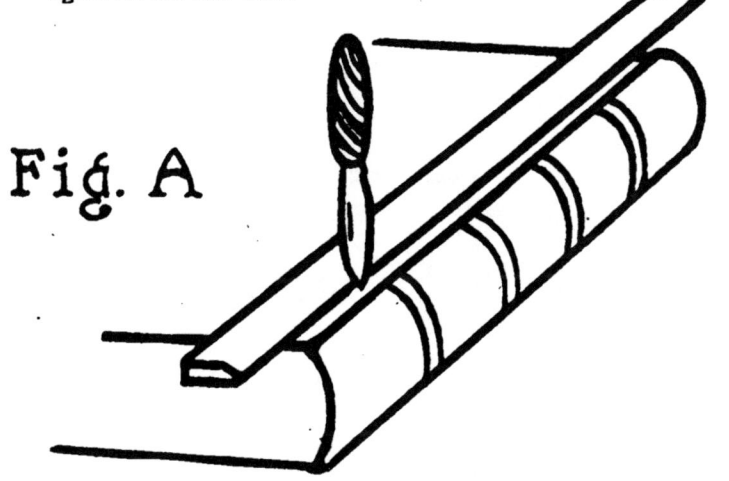

Fig. A

All the leather on the back and over the hinges, up to the cut above mentioned, should then be lifted or scraped off. As a majority of old books are bound with the leather glued directly to the lining of the back, a certain amount of the old glue, according to its condition, scraped smooth, should be left on the lining.

While old calf backs are generally so dry that they must be scraped off in pieces, it is sometimes possible, when the back is of more solid leather, to remove the old back, with the label and gilding, in one piece. If this can be done, the inside of the old back should be scraped and this back pasted on again over the new leather back. This is, of course, preferable, as by this means more of the characteristics of the old cover are preserved.

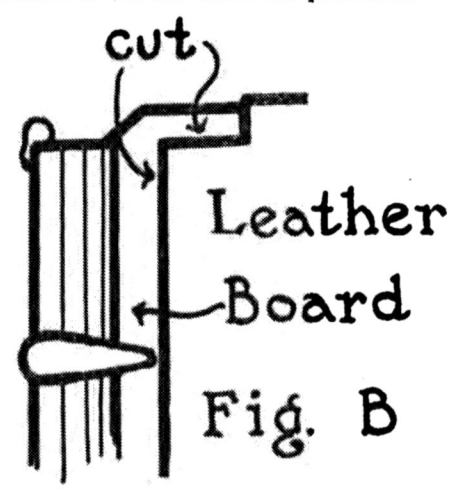

Fig. B

When the back is clear of leather, a small cut about half an inch long is made at the top and bottom of each side, at the ends of, and at right angles to, the first cut; from the ends of the short cuts, the leather is again cut at right angles over the top and bottom edges of the boards. (Fig. B.) As these points, near the top and bottom of the inside hinges, the end-papers pasted on the inside of the boards are lifted for a short distance so that all the old leather under them can be removed.

The head-bands should then be examined to see that they are firmly in place and any missing band replaced, the new band being simply glued to the back lining.

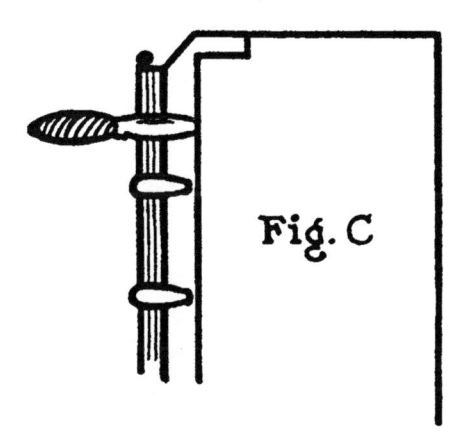

Fig. C

A sharp, thin knife is then run under the leather of the sides, following the first long cut, loosening this leather from the boards for about half an inch back from the cut, this distance equalling the short cuts at top and bottom. (Fig. C.)

The book is now ready for the new back. This is cut from the leather to be used, in width equal to the distance over the back and hinges plus a trifle less than half an inch on each side, and in height to project half an inch beyond the top and bottom of the book.

This leather is then pared thin on the inside for about half an inch all around the edge. Paring requires careful

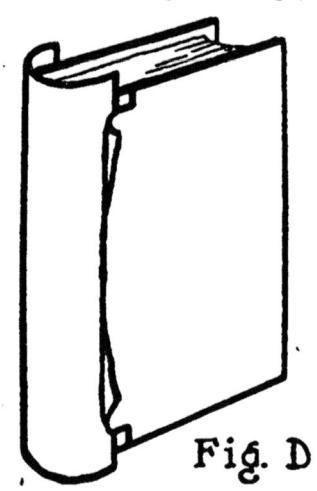

Fig. D

work and a sharp knife, otherwise the piece may not be pared thin enough to set smoothly, or may be cut through and ruined.

The back lining of the book itself, and the inside of the new back, are then given a medium thin coat of paste, and the leather set evenly in place. The side edges of the back are slipped under the leather of the sides where this leather was loosened from the boards following the first, long cut, and pasted directly on the boards. (Fig. D.) By this time the paste on the top and bottom ends of the back will be dry. These are given another coat of paste, one at a time, and turned under upon themselves, starting in the middle, the corners being carried over the edges of

Fig. E.

the boards and securely pasted down inside where the end papers have been pushed back. The top, beyond the boards, is tucked in behind the head-band. When the top and bottom of the back have been treated in this way, they are then flattened with a folder and the edges of the hinges are bent in to form the head-cap finish observable on almost any book bound by hand in leather. (Fig. E.) The tops of the head-bands may require a slight touch of paste so that the leather turned over upon them will stay in place.

The inside end papers, where they were lifted at the top and bottom near hinges, are then pasted down over the corners of the new back which are folded in at these points, and the leather lifted from the sides is pasted down over the side edges of the new back where these are pasted directly on the boards. New inside hinges of paper or cloth may be added, if required; but if these are to go in they are best set in place before the new back is pasted on.

The new back being in place, it might be given a certain amount of finish. If the book is sewn on outside cords, these will show as raised bands on the back, and the new leather is, of course, moulded over these when it is first set in place. In such a case, a satisfactory, plain finish can be obtained by moulding these bands distinctly. This is done by running the edge of the folder in the angle at each side of each band with a see-saw motion. Experiment will show how this may give a smooth, polished line on each side of the bands if it is thoroughly done with fair pressure while the leather is still moist from the paste on the inside. Before attempting any such operations, however, the outside of the new back must be washed entirely free from any spots of paste.

An additional "blind" line may be made at top and bottom across the back, by bending over the back a straight piece of vellum to serve as a guide to the folder. A smooth back without bands may be finished with a series of double or single lines put on in this manner, care being taken that the line of the vellum guide is at right angles to the side edges of the back.

The back of the old label, if this is to be used again, is then scraped and the label pasted on in its proper place between bands; or a new label, properly lettered in gilt, may be ordered from a binder.

The entire work, when almost dry, should be pressed over with a hot flat-iron to press down any irregularities, the edges of the cut leather on the sides, and the top and bottom finish over head-bands. The iron must be well warmed rather than hot. If too hot, it will lift the surface of the leather. The book should then be placed under pressure to dry.

For the operation of rebacking one needs only a sharp, thin knife, a ruler or straight edge, a bone folder and a small flat-iron in the way of tools. A small press is desirable, but not necessary. The folder, which may be

Fig. F

purchased from a dealer in bookbinders' supplies, will be furnished with square ends; one of these ends should be sawed off on an angle and smoothed with a file to give a pointed end, which will be found very useful. (Fig. F.) The flat-iron should be wedge-shaped, about four inches long, with straight, rounded edges. (Fig. G.) Irons of this kind may be found in toy shops, and will be found extremely useful and easy to handle in all small repair operations.

To the above tools may be added, if desired, one or two small tooling irons of simple design for blind tooling. Such irons are used just hot enough to hiss very slightly

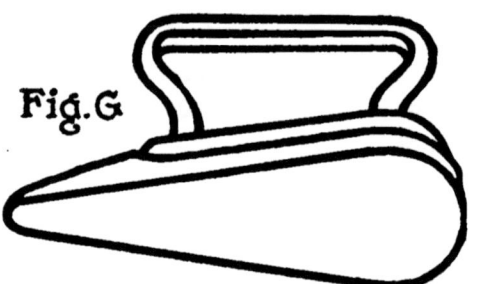

Fig. G

when touched with a wet cloth, and are pressed firmly and evenly on the leather for two or three seconds to leave a good impression.

Books bound in boards, with cloth or paper backs, may be rebacked with cloth, parchment, or even with heavy paper in facsimile of the original back. In the latter case, it is advisable to line the back with a strip of Japan vellum, which should extend over upon the boards under the new paper back. Parchment is often satisfactory and requires no paring, but must be handled carefully when damp from paste, or it will stretch out of shape.

CHAPTER IV
REPAIRING OLD BINDINGS
Translated From Bonnardot

MODERN LEVANT BINDING

Not having the secret of that special, certain skill which produces flexible and artistic bindings, I am obliged to advise amateurs who wish to see their books reclad in princely mantles, to apply to our able Parisian binders. But I can give, from my own experience, some good suggestions to amateurs on the manner of cleaning, repairing and freshening ordinary morocco bindings, and also, under certain conditions, those sumptuous moroccos of the Levant, the mere perfume of which fascinates all true-born bibliophiles.

CLEANING THE COVER. It is possible, without being obliged to touch the boards of a book, to clean and repair the covering, either entirely or in spots. To accomplish this, I know some methods which are simple and practical, although, of course, too imperfect to restore to an ancient binding all the brightness and vigor of its youth. A rather mature prima-donna may, perhaps, within certain limits, soften the ravages of time; but, when observed closely, the lines on her face cannot be concealed. And this is also the case with the coquettish old bindings of which I speak.

Morocco or calf which has become soiled by constant handling may be cleaned with a fine sponge dipped in a jelly of white soap. If there are spots of oil or grease, this soap will not suffice; it will be necessary to use black soap, or perhaps a weak solution of some alkali, such as potash or ammonia. In using such alkalis, it is best to first try them on some odd pieces of leather of the same color or upon some part of the bindings not likely to be noticed, because certain colors in leather are apt to decompose or change their tint under the action of an alkali. It has been observed that alkalis tend to darken the leather, more or less; therefore, after employing them, a little acidified water must be applied to neutralize their effect. Also that morocco should be moistened only very slightly, as, otherwise, the surface grain may be smoothed away.

One might begin by trying benzine; this liquid will not attack any color or, at least, only a color formed principally of fatty or resinous substances. Benzine does not act like an alkali; it does not saponify the greasy body, but it dissolves it as water dissolves a salt, a gum or gelatine. It must be used quickly, as it evaporates much more rapidly than ammonia, which itself is considered volatile. The latter will mix with water, but benzine combines only with alcohol.

Thus benzine, like all other essential oils, operates only as a dissolvent and, after having been applied, either pure or mixed with alcohol, upon the book cover, it must be wiped off with a soft cloth before it evaporates, so that the particles of grease which it has dissolved, but not decomposed, will not sink again into the leather and later reappear on its surface.

The best method, after having poured some drops of the liquid upon one side of the book, is to turn this side toward the ground. In this position the benzine, charged with part of the greasy substance, will run down and accumulate upon the lowest edge of the cover, from which it can quickly be wiped off with the substances it holds in solution. Perhaps an even better method of operation may be discovered.

This manner of employing benzine, alcohol or turpentine as dissolvents for the greasy body is equally applicable for removing oily spots from prints, and I recommend it to the reader for experiment. When grease is removed with alkaline water, it is useless to proceed in this manner; the soapy substance which forms on the leather after rubbing should be removed with a damp sponge, after which the book should be dried in the air and then placed under pressure.

Fresh spots of oil or grease may sometimes be removed by impalpable powders of some clay-like nature, absorbent and slightly alkaline.

A spot of ordinary black ink upon morocco, sheepskin, calf or smooth parchment, loses its color when touched with a few drops of sorrel salt or oxalic acid; but I will repeat here the advice already given that these substances may alter certain colors and that it is best to first try them on extra pieces of leather. If the tint lightens or changes only slightly, the spot can be retoned and brightened simply with properly mixed water-colors, after having neutralized, with an alkali, the traces of the acid.

The yellowish spot which remains after the black ink has disappeared is not very noticeable upon brown or yellowish skins, but on vellum or parchment it is more or less apparent. How can this be removed? For if one is obliged to prolong the action of the oxalic acid on the iron oxide which causes it, this portion of the skin not only loses its gloss, but also becomes subject to a more or less rapid process of dissolution. (*)

(*) Bonnardot, at this point, discusses in considerable detail various opinions as to the removal of these iron oxide stains, but without coming to any definite conclusion except that they are "of all stains, the most tenacious." Experiments in chemistry, especially upon any binding of value, should not be lightly undertaken. The use of water-colors for retinting the spot of yellowish bleach might be tried with more safety and a greater possibility of success. M. S. B.

When the spots are of Chinese ink, old or recent, and have sunk into the texture, as sometimes happens, they resist all known agents.

Most of the old bindings which have been long exposed for sale on the parapets of our quays, have been at one moment roasted by an ardent sun and at the next distended by a damp atmosphere; they have, therefore, contracted "skin troubles" more or less curable according to the duration of their ordeal. The gentler regimen of the bookshelves, placed in a room where the temperature is more nearly uniform, sometimes suffices to restore their warped covers; but when the surface of the leather has fallen off in scales, carrying away the gold tooling, it is better, if they are worthy of it, to deliver them to the binder for new covers; that is, of course, when the paper, the essential organ of their existence, is not musty beyond recovery. If the paper is in bad shape, the book is lost or, at least, is beyond giving pleasure to a bibliophile; it resembles a very old man attacked by an incurable disease; it is useful only for reference.

Some books, placed in less rude conditions, have only the skin stripped here and there by contact with rougher neighbors trimmed with nails or clasps, with hard boards or with wicker-work, but movement against these objects might ruin an entire library in a single day. The library of the Louvre, it might be mentioned, was being moved last spring to a new location, by means of these wicker baskets so formidable despite the straw or oakum with which they were lined. Some of my own books have passed several times through this fatal ordeal and have suffered greatly from it. Now when I change my residence I use, with rather tardy precaution, well-planed boxes.

Books slightly roughened, their bloom destroyed simply by friction, may be freshened and restored to an aspect of health to conceal, up to a certain point, the wear of their old coverings. With an old glove one may spread over their surface a little flour paste or fairly thick starch to which a little alum might be added. This is smeared quickly over the back, sides and edges of the boards, and the surplus wiped off with a soft cloth. This carries away any dust which may have been deposited and also soilings which soften in the moisture. (*)

After this operation, there will remain on the volume a thin coating of gelatine or of gluten (the viscous part of the starch). Before this has entirely dried, it should be thoroughly wiped over with the palm of the hand. Any scraped portions of the leather will have a dull appearance and will sometimes show darker than other parts of the cover. The edges of stripped or broken spots may be

(*) Certain bindings of the sixteenth century have on their covers designs in tint formed simply of water colors. In such cases, the flour paste should not be used, or else the designs should first be accurately traced so that they can be restored, if necessary, after the operation.

refastened to the cover by means of the starch sizing. The corners which, nearly always, will be found worn or bent, may be straightened and strengthened. In a word, if the cover cannot be restored to pass as new, it may at least be rendered more presentable and made to contrast more favorably with other books it may meet upon the shelf.

After a washing with starch, as after cleaning with alkalis, it often happens that the covers of a book are dulled. Their polish, where the bloom has not been worn away, can be restored by rubbing with a piece of flannel moistened with a few drops of very siccative varnish (purchased from art dealers or dealers in bookbinders' materials).

Most amateurs and binders know this inexpensive way of restoring a certain lustre to faded and erupted, if one may use that expression, bindings. If I have spoken rather in detail, it is for the sake of amateurs still inexperienced or living in a small, provincial town. As these latter probably would not know where to procure varnish, I offer the recipe of M. F. Mairet, which indicates the proportions for a large quantity but which may be divided by ten. In the thirty-ninth part of his "Essay Upon Binding" he says: Dissolve eight ounces of sandarach (resin), two ounces of mastic in drops, eight ounces of gum-lac in tablets and two ounces of Venetian turpentine, in three litres (quarts) of spirits of wine at a temperature of thirty-six to forty degrees. (*). Crush the gums and, to completely dissolve them, place the bottle which contains them in the wine, in hot water, shaking it from time to time. This varnish can be preserved in the bottle in which it is made, keeping the bottle tightly corked. When one wishes to use the varnish, the bottle should not be shaken because of the deposit which forms.

I will here make a recommendation analogous to that of M. Le Normand; it is desirable to place the glass bottle in a basin containing warm water before placing it in the very hot water, as otherwise it may break. Also, instead of shaking the bottle, the contents may be stirred with a glass rod.

This is how M. Mairet describes the use of his varnish; with a very soft brush, the varnish is spread over the covers of the book without putting it on the gilding. When it is nearly dry, it is polished with a piece of white cloth slightly moistened with olive oil. It should first be rubbed gently, then with more force as the varnish dries. For complete success it is essential that the covers be perfectly dry (†) and without the slightest dampness.

Instead of using this varnish, one may give a fair polish which, however, is not so enduring, by coating with the liquid known as "glaire." This is made from the white of an egg beaten up with a little water and

(*) Centigrade, i. e. ninety-seven to one hundred and four degrees Fahrenheit.   M. S. B.
(†) At the beginning.   M. S. B.

alcohol. (*) One might also try a glaze made with hide glue or gum-arabic.

The lustre of white vellum or of calf, when they have not been badly rubbed by use, may be restored by rubbing with an agate burnisher, a polished bone or a curved iron slightly warmed. Sometimes, before polishing, according to M. Le Normand, the covers should be rubbed with flannel holding a little tallow or walnut oil. (†) Great care should be taken in polishing morocco, whether genuine or imitation, in order that the grain which contributes so much to its beauty may not be rubbed away. The surface of sheep also, which is a very delicate leather, is easily stripped. To polish leathers such as these, binders' varnish or, at least, the glaire mentioned above, should be used.

REPAIRING HOLES AND BROKEN SURFACES. We will now consider any serious wounds which go deeper than the surface of the leather. One often sees covers of calf, sheep or morocco deeply stripped or even pierced like the coats of Diogenes and Ruy-Blas; the back,

---

(*) The best modern practice in making glaire is to beat up the white of an egg with about half its quantity of vinegar, allowing the mixture to stand over night. This mixture, covered, will keep for several days, or until it gets thick and cloudy. M. S. B.

(†) Unbroken surfaces of white vellum can easily be cleaned with a soft pencil-eraser. A vellum binding which is "tacky" may be rubbed over with powdered soapstone after cleaning.
M. S. B.

the sides and corners, especially the lower ones, broken away even to the point of exposing the boards. This is a state of cynicism which calls for some remedy; the simple smearing on of starch is powerless to heal such damages.

It is often possible to restore missing fragments by means of new pieces of the same kind and tint of leather. I will assume that the amateur possesses a collection of odd scraps of morocco, brown calf, old vellum, etc., removed with more or less right from books whose pages have been unfortunately ruined, to be devoted to more humiliating uses. These should be searched for a suitable piece; sometimes this is found. The essential point is to match the grain of the leather. When the tint is too light, it can easily be darkened with water-colors; when it is too dark, one must search further. One may, however, lighten a little piece of calf which is too dark by means of very weak acid.

Suppose the desired patch found. The hole or broken place in the cover is cleaned and the edge cut sharp to prevent further tearing, and in this is set a piece from the patch, cut exactly to fit. If the amateur has not time to do this careful mosaic patching, he may, with a small, thin blade, raise the edges of the leather about the hole and, applying paste or glue directly to the board, slip in a patch piece which has been roughly cut a little larger than the hole and pared thin around the edges. The edges of the hole should then be moistened with paste and firmly pressed down into place over the patch. A patch made in this way is less agreeable to the eye than when made by the first process, for by this latter method there always remains a sort of raised pad which accents the form of the hole.

Let us consider now the repair of bruises, more or less deep, caused by rough contact with some hard, sharp or rough body.

When the stripped parts are still hanging to the cover, they should be straightened out and pressed back into place after being given a light coat of thick starch paste. But if the stripped parts corresponding to the bruise are missing, how shall the furrow, which reveals a spongy appearance, be brought up level with the surface of the cover? With a corresponding patch inserted in the fissure? This is an operation, I think, very difficult to carry out, and it is simpler to cut the furrow into a definite hole if one wishes to proceed in this way. Let us try and imagine some kind of putty for such repairs.

I do not wish to write hastily of any method of procedure for the fabrication of bruised leather, but it seems to me that a paste or putty formed of powdered or shredded leather, boiled with a little flour paste, would answer our purpose. With this one could fill up the furrow and then, when the paste has dried, scrape off the excess surface and burnish the dried inlay. This method should answer very well, but there is still another which

I have tried, although it is not so delicate. I employed flour paste mixed simply with Spanish white (*). With this, I puttied up my book like a picture in process of being retouched. I even succeeded, with this paste, in imitating the grain of the morocco. I tinted the patches by applying color mixed with gum. But this sort of repair is only applicable to parts of the cover away from the edges; in the neighborhood of the hinges, this unelastic paste will break loose or, at least, render the book difficult to open.

I experimented also with gutta-percha. This brownish substance has the property, at a certain temperature (towards seventy degrees) (†) of melting and adhering to the leather and, on cooling, recovers its natural, semi-elastic state. But after having been melted at a fire or, if the season is right, by sunlight through a lens, it turns brown and will not harmonize in tint except with very dark calf, and I have found no method of lightening it.

We will now speak of repairing and patching the cover in those parts which serve as hinges. This is an operation practicable only when a substance very thin and supple can be found. I have succeeded in restoring this part of a book by using a strip of gold-beaters skin, slipped between the back and the side and fastened, on one part, to the edge of the side and, on the other, to the boards

(*) Whiting (chalk) used as a pigment.   M. S. B.
(†) One hundred and fifty-eight degrees Fahrenheit.
                                                        M. S. B.

lining the back. I then gave to this skin a tint corresponding to that of the cover. The break remained visible; I only reconnected the parts so that the book could be opened and closed. (*)

Would one succeed better by using a thin piece of rubber? I have never tried this, but this substance, I believe, could not be obtained in very thin sheets except by being considerably stretched, a process which would soon destroy the elasticity which is its essential quality. Perhaps the broken hinges of a dark calf book could be joined without great difficulty by means of the liquefied gutta-percha mentioned above.

I have sometimes repaired the corners of a volume with more or less success. In cases where the damage was slight, after having loosened the paper on the inside of the cover at the corner, either with, or without, moistening

(*) This operation does not seem entirely clear, but the idea is evidently to fold a thin strip of the skin into a "V" shape, inserting the strip, folded edge up or down, as the condition of the hinge may require, into the broken hinge all along its length, gluing the arms of the "V," one to the back and one to the cover to form a new, folded hinge. The operator will probably find, however, that when the hinges of a book are broken through a better and more lasting procedure is to reback the book. Gold-beaters skin is the outside membrane of the large intestine of the ox, properly prepared. Where the hinges of a book are broken, it is better to provide new leather hinges, using strips about half an inch wide slipped in under the broken edges and carried over the edge of the boards at top and bottom. Raise the broken edges, for the proper distance, from back and boards, and paste down again over the new hinge.   M. S. B.

it, I pushed back the damaged skin for a short distance, then glued upon the board over the corner a fragment of leather of the same kind and tint, pared thin, then pressed down the rough edges and fashioned the new corner by moistening the leather. Then, having replaced the broken edges of the original leather, I recolored the patch to an exact match. (*)

When the leather at the corner is entirely dilapidated an entirely new corner of triangular form should be supplied, pasted down level with the leather on the cover, which has been cut away smoothly where the new corner is joined on. If the corner of the board is itself tattered, it can be stiffened by the use of paste or glue, thoroughly soaked in and left to dry. A little Spanish white might be added to the paste to give it more solidity.

But when the angle of the corner is entirely rounded, weakened and demolished by use, it should be renewed by incorporating an entirely new corner on the board. To fasten this securely, the edge of the board should be cut across at an angle of forty-five degrees, then split, and the upper half cut away for a short distance back. The new triangular piece for the corner is also notched underneath

(*) To prevent wear on the lower corners and edges of books in the library, strips of velvet may be laid along the shelves under the books. If this is done, the little extra care required in removing and replacing the books without wrinkling up the velvet will be more than offset by the protection which the velvet gives. M. S. B.

to correspond so that the two patches will superimpose and exactly fit. Here one makes use of strong paste or glue. This operation is not difficult but it requires time and patience, for a considerable amount of leather must be raised from the board and then replaced. If one is not endowed with patience, it is better to turn this work over to a binder, otherwise one will work to no purpose and will damage his book instead of restoring it.

REPAIRING EDGES. To remove a spot of ink or color from the edges of a book, the substance described for similar operations on pages or prints may be used. However, there is this distinction; here one is not concerned with the surface of a single sheet but with a great many page-edges one after another. If the edges to be cleaned are not placed under pressure, the liquids, penetrating between them, will stain the pages themselves. If, however, the ink itself has thus spread into the pages, it might be desirable to send the dissolving liquid over the same route. In this case, it will be necessary to efface from each page the moisture following the application of the remedy, and this requires careful work.

If, on the contrary, the spot soils merely the surface of the edges, the volume should be placed under pressure in such a position that the edges to be cleaned stand vertical; then, with a small brush, the necessary liquid may be applied. The spot removed (supposing that it is of a nature which may be decomposed) it is necessary, in some cases, to restore the general tint of the edges; this is not a very difficult matter, at least when they are not marbled. When the edges are gilt, the gold is not usually attacked and naturally resists the action of the chemical agents; the ink or other spot can thus be removed without necessitating the restoration of the gold afterward. A spot may sometimes be removed with a dampened sponge. (*) Even Chinese ink, a black which will not decompose, is often susceptible to this gentle procedure by means of which it may be wiped away.

Let us now suppose that the edges are free from spots but that they are faded, and partly discolored. It is easy enough to brighten the colors if they are not too complicated; I will add; and provided the pages are not unequal, with some advanced and some drawn back, destroying the general level, for, in this case, it is necessary to begin by repairing the back without separating the volume; an almost impossible operation. (†) The color brightened, it may be repolished with an agate burnisher while the edges are held closely pressed together. If edges, not colored, but gilt, have been damaged here and there by use, perfect restoration is impracticable. A new patch of gold applied over the worn spot contrasts in

(*) Gilding, especially if modern, is apt to soften and come off if rubbed with water. M. S. B.

(†) See my remarks on lining up with Japan vellum in the chapter on *General Restoration*. M. S. B.

freshness and polish with the rest of the surface and, at the points where it necessarily overlaps the perfect parts, the excess gold remains noticeable. Undoubtedly, the best procedure is to have the whole surface regilded by a prefessional gilder.

If one has gone to the trouble of brightening the edges, one may desire to complete the restoration by renewing the head-bands. I have never had patience enough to make a head-band, a kind of needle-work which belongs particularly to the bookbinders' trade. The amateur should have recourse to a binder for this or, if he wishes to attempt the work himself, consult any of the books published on binding.

RESTORING THE GILDING. (*) It is sometimes necessary to brighten, patch and partially replace the gilt ornaments of a precious book. In cleaning a book, as I have described above, with soap-jelly or starch paste, the gold is not affected if the operation is carried out according to directions; on the contrary, one lifts from the gold the deposit of dirt which deadens its brilliancy. But if it has been, at some points, destroyed by the breaks in the leather,

(*) In this place, Bonnardot gives a few simple suggestions for repairing broken fragments of the gold tooling. The amateur is cautioned not to attempt the application of hot gilding tools and gold leaf to any binding for which he has any regard unless he has carefully prepared himself by thoroughly studying the detailed directions for this work which may be found in text-books on binding, and by extensive practice on odd pieces of various leathers. M. S. B.

it is necessary, in order to restore the gold, to refinish the leather at the broken point. Here a considerable difficulty presents itself, and it is necessary to find a filler which will serve as a base. Gutta-percha will not answer at such points, except for cold gilding, as the application of a warm gilding iron would liquefy it. The only satisfactory solution is to inlay with leather.

I have sometimes succeeded in restoring missing spots of gilding by the simple employment of gilt paint, laid with a fine brush upon the properly prepared patch, imitating carefully each missing part of the ornamentation. This kind of joining, however, lacks brilliance and solidity; wiping with a damp sponge is sufficient to effact it; but it may be given a little more permanency by a coat of binders' varnish.

I can suggest a less imperfect method of procedure. Where there are thin lines or figures such as circles to join, the amateur can do this with home-made tools. Such tools may be made of small brass wire, some straight edges and others curved like gouges. (*) He should also have small dots of various sizes, circular or oval in profile. With these simple elements, most line designs may be patched. The ground properly prepared, the warm iron tool to be used is applied upon fragments of gold-leaf.

(*) All set, of course, in wooden or pottery handles. Wooden handles for such tools, or the tools themselves, may be procured at moderate prices from dealers in bookbinders' materials.

M. S. B.

The iron should be a little hotter than boiling water; otherwise it will not fix the gold in place. If too hot, it will burn the leather. Gilders test the heat of an iron by touching it with a wet finger, and are able to tell, by the sizzle and amount of vapor given off, whether the degree of heat is right. A more simple method, for the amateur, is to try the iron on a fragment of leather. (*) The excess of gold not pressed in by the iron may be wiped off with a fragment of woolen cloth.

If it is necessary to restore a complicated ornament upon an ancient and very precious binding, special irons must be cut, using the tooling still in place as a guide. With patience and skill, one may fashion these for himself. The required ornamentation is traced from another spot where it is still intact on the binding, with a brush holding resin varnish or wax. This tracing, which naturally leaves an imprint in reverse, is applied to a piece of copper, and the design retouched on the copper

---

(*) The impression should first be made on the leather by the hot tool, without gold, and painted wtih glaire. When the glaire is nearly dry, a fragment of gold-leaf is picked up on a pad of cotton wool slightly touched with cocoanut oil and pressed down on the blind impression of the tool. The tool is then pressed into its former impression, setting the gold. The process is very delicate; the tool must be perfectly clean and the gold-leaf, which is very difficult to handle, worked from a padded cloth dusted with brick-dust, or a similar substance, to prevent the leaf from adhering there while it is being cut to the proper size. M. S. B.

with the same varnish or wax. (*) The other faces of the cube or cylinder of copper used are coated, and the copper placed in a bath of azotic acid. The acid will eat the metal not protected as above, leaving the ornament standing out in relief, something after the manner of a stereotype plate. Or, the electro-chemical procedure of stereotyping may be used to the same end.

By the aid of a form obtained in some such manner as the above, it is possible to restore the effaced ornaments, provided that the leather is prepared to receive and hold the gold. Let me note in passing that it is difficult for inexperienced amateurs to set gold smoothly; only long practice will make this possible. Necessarily, the very thin gold leaf always covers and reaches beyond the spot to be tooled. It is essential that the iron be pressed exactly upon the spot intended to receive it, which is very difficult to accomplish. Moreover, the gold must be kept smooth and fresh over the entire impression. Perhaps one might substitute for the gold leaf a coat of gold powder spread over the design, which should be coated with albuminous paste (glaire) to hold the powder.

One sometimes wishes, also, to rectify a defective title or erroneous date on the binding. The simplest method is to stamp the desired lettering or date on an odd bit of leather, which is then applied to the book. The amateur

(*) Wax would, of course, be used hot. M. S. B.

may do this himself if he has the necessary letter, a form to hold them, and a certain amount of skill.

Suppose a case where, in a title anciently gilt and which one wishes to preserve, there is a single letter or a single character to change. It is first necessary to efface the letter or character to be replaced. To do this, it is touched with a drop of alcohol; on wiping it, the varnish which may have covered the gold is removed. If the gold resists thorough rubbing, chemical compositions may be tried. I would not advise, however, the use of aqua-regia, the infallible dissolvent of gold, because it would disorganize the leather. I think that a drop of mercury, applied hot upon a letter by means of an iron or sun-rays through a lens, would absorb and amalgamate the metallic particles. In any case, there would still remain a moulded impression which might be removed, I think, by swelling the leather at that spot by means of a jet of steam applied through a very narrow glass tube. (*)

The impression effaced, or at least reduced, one may proceed to replace the corrected letter. For this, a letter or figure matching the others in size and character must be secured. Sometimes it is necessary for the amateur to make this himself. This can be done by securing a

(*) As mentioned in a note above, gold may often be loosened by merely removing the varnish and thoroughly moistening with water, after which the metal may be coaxed out with a thin, smooth, wooden splinter, preferably wound on the end with a bit of cotton wool. M. S. B.

fragment of rolled copper and, with the aid of small pincers, fashioning the profile of the desired letter on its edge. The thickness of the metal would form the thickness of the letter's face; strokes required slender may be pared with a knife. With a little care and skill, the desired character may be produced. The bit of metal is then set in a handle of plaster or clay, which is allowed to dry and harden.

TRANSFERRING ANCIENT COVERS. Is it possible to transfer the covers of works richly bound, but valueless inside, to the boards of other books more precious in their text and more deserving of the transferred binding? Some of our binders have replied in the affirmative.

Many a volume has retained virginal the splendour of its original binding simply because the text has been tiresome and insipid. In this class appear certain volumes of indigestible theology, "Sacred works and not to be touched," as Voltaire remarked, and those odes of court-flattery, insipidly rhymed in doggerel, in aristocratic liveries, addressed to high personages who paid for them but who never read them. From books of such sorts, one may, without remorse, lift the precious coverings. However, to make use of them, it is necessary that all their dimensions correspond with the new volumes on which it is proposed to place them. The old books in good condition are easily despoiled when there is no need to be careful of the cording, the fly leaves or the boards. The process requiring the most time is that of scraping away the dry paste which adheres here and there to the inside of the leather after its removal. I have re-covered more than one quarto in covers of gold tooled vellum lifted from books of the same format. When the back was too narrow or too wide, I replaced this part, but then the cover was formed of three pieces. When the back was of the right width, I effaced the old title, generally lettered in ink, by means of sorrel-salt, and inscribed the new title in the same place but with Chinese ink. Where the old title happened to be gilt, I covered it with a new piece of skin, finding it too laborious to efface all the letters by the process mentioned above.

Let us suppose it is necessary to replace upon a rare volume, changing only the boards, the old contemporary binding which covered it. If the skin is worn on the edges and corners and at the hinges, removing it without injury from the old boards is a very delicate operation. However, it may be done, even without moistening the leather, by using the skill and patience which both come from practice. Our binders, in cases where expense has not been in consideration, have executed more than one feat of this kind. Only, nearly always, they are obliged to renew the parts injured by use and the end papers. They apply, here and there, to the new boards bits of leather matching the tint of the old, reset the preserved cover, still charged with the rich ornaments which constitute its value and, upon the portions renewed, restore the gilding after the model of that which they have before them. More than one binder has succeeded, with great skill, in placing upon a new foundation the splendid cover of a very rare book without being obliged to go to the regrettable extreme of a second sewing and trimming. It is even possible, with the exercise of great care, to clean the sheets, one by one, and repair the torn and missing places, without separating the book; but one can see that such restorations are a matter of expense and not suitable except for books of considerable value. I believe that there exist in Paris binders of sufficient skill to replace a cover "in octavo," transposing it without injury to the volume and without leaving the least trace of this difficult operation.

CHAPTER V
REBINDING

SOLANDER SLIP-CASE

In Chapter Thirteen of his *Essai,* Bonnardot remarks:

"When one sees upon the table in a public shop, a rare book roughly sewn, ignobly deteriorated and, especially, badly cut down, either too much or unevenly, one may believe that it has passed, at some period, through the hands of a provincial bookbinder or of one of our Parisian binders of the lower order, who consider it proper to wrap up a typographical monument of the Louis XII period in a way to strike off about nineteen-twentieths of its value.

"I know of no species of vandals worse, more primitive or more irresponsible than these botchers. But one can see how they are sometimes impelled, in spite of a natural taste, to commit these ravages. After considerable discussion, a person may offer them about 75 centimes ($0.15), more or less, for a piece of work which, if done with care, should well be worth eight or ten times that amount. The natural and inevitable punishment caused by this penny-pinching, is the almost total depreciation of a book placed in the care of an easy-going bibliophile who, with a light heart condemns his old friend to a binding limited in price to 75 centimes.

"The provincial bookbinder whose work, with its dirty, warped boards, simpers under a covering of sheep still hairy and spotted with patches of ink, is in much the same class as a cheap glazer and gilder to whom an amateur iconophile might naively send for restoration a rare Albert Durer; and both these similar to an architect who, with blind decision, would be sent to mutilate the flanks of some majestic cathedral. This redoubtable trio, born enemies of souvenirs engraved in stone or upon paper, botch and destroy, although perhaps without malice, at least three-fourths of anything on which they operate. May these tardy remarks still save something from the ruins!

"The most irremediable of the crimes which can be committed in rebinding a small, old book, is the trimming of margins. The simple matter of a centime's economy in the size of the boards, may direct the trimming of some charming gothic quarto up to the very text. One may thrice exclaim with joy when the text itself has not been cropped. Those who partly realize, or divine by instinct, that margins are good for something, sometimes take pains to preserve them, but trim them with an inequality so shocking that the victim has only escaped Charybdis in order to fall upon Scylla. Undoubtedly, the greatest merit of a rare book is to have untrimmed margins or, at least, margins trimmed only slightly and evenly. But to obtain evenness, it is not proper to cut huge slices in order to square the edges; such zeal for symmetry easily might result in cutting into the text. The best method for squaring a book which was unevenly cut when previously bound, is to refold and equalize each sheet before any further trimming is done; a long and detailed operation for which one pays, not in centimes but in francs."

Bonnardot goes on from the above, very pointed remarks, to describe various operations of rebinding, with an idea of assisting bibliophiles who are too far from the centres of civilization to get in touch with a good binder. For detailed information along these lines, which hardly come within the scope of the present volume, books written especially on the subject of binding should be consulted.

It is very difficult to execute a satisfactory binding without going through a long period of practice and apprenticeship. And this work not only includes several long and dreary operations, such as sewing, which the average bibliophile would not have the time or patience to undertake, but also requires a number of bulky tools and presses, out of place except in a shop or work-room. Any book in serious need of rebinding is better placed in the hands of an experienced binder, preferably one who specializes in individual bindings. With the book, written directions may be sent, when distance renders personal consultation impossible.

As nine-tenths of all binders, even today, still practice many careless methods against which bibliophiles have protested for centuries, it is desirable, in any case, both as a precaution and as a practical help and reminder to the binder, to furnish, with each book to be bound, complete written instructions for the work. With the written directions, a sketch of the book may be furnished, giving details of the design of tooling wanted, except in cases where it is known that this matter may safely be left to the good taste of the binder. If many books are sent to the same binder, however, suggestions on finish and tooling may very well be made. Sometimes these may prove of interest to the binder himself. The reason for such suggestions is that nearly every binder has certain set personal conventions, especially in the matter of tooling construction, causing, in all his bindings, a certain uniformity of design. Although this may be varied by the different selection of the actual tools used and the colors of the leather, it becomes monotonous in its general construction and damages the visible personality of the individual volumes.

A form of direction sheet, which will, of course, vary with varying requirements, follows.

TITLE. In gilt on back.

THE
ENEMIES
OF
BOOKS

William
Blades

DATE. In gilt at bottom of back. 1880

COVER. Full, dark brown pebbled morocco, best quality Turkey. Full grain, not crushed.

TOP. Gilt top. Please trim as little as possible.

EDGES. Do not trim or cut bottom or fore edges. (*)

TOOLING. Gilt line borders on sides near edges, with corner ornaments; use geometrical design ornaments if you have them, rather than flowers. Panels on back.

SEWING. Sew flexible on flat bands with leather back glued direct to the lining of signatures. Please do

(*) Or: Gilt edges. (This requires, in many cases, considerable trimming all around.) Or: Bottom and fore edges gilt on uncut edges. (This is a more expensive process and a rather delicate one. It is not in general use.)

not saw into backs of signatures for bands or cords. (*)

END PAPERS. Plain light brown or white. (†)

SPECIAL. Be sure and place clean sheets of paper over the etched illustrations whenever the book is in press. The original wrappers now on are considerably torn and are very brittle. Please mount these as well as you can, on thin, strong paper, and bind them in at the back.

The price for this work may be agreed on beforehand, but it is better left to the binder, in order that he will not feel cramped, should the necessity of a little unforeseen work develop. Whatever their other failings may be, binders are generally honest in such matters and are not likely to overcharge, especially on average work.

(*) It is often difficult to persuade a binder to sew on flat bands or outside cords. The usual, and easiest method is to saw into the backs of the signatures and lay the cords in the "V" shaped cut thus made. This method of sewing should be protested against unless the book has already been so treated in a former binding and no additional cutting is required. Most of the raised bands found on modern bindings are "false," being in no way an essential part of the binding and serving no practical purpose. Even their use as guides for decoration is doubtful, as they tend to unnecessary convention.

(†) On a valuable book in an expensive binding, the end papers should be sewn in. This means extra trouble for the binder and calls for a little extra charge. End papers are very seldom sewn in on modern bindings, although often so secured in bindings of a century or two ago.

This may be a good place to remark, perhaps needlessly, that valuable books, particularly first editions, should always be retained in their original covers, whether cloth, boards or leather, whenever this is at all practicable. Ancient books in their original calf or sheep, but with broken backs or hinges, and requiring attention for their proper preservation, should be rebacked rather than rebound.

The reasons for this are numerous. Principally, the fact that a book is still in its original binding is a fair guarantee that it has not been trimmed since it originally left the binder's hands. It often happens, also, that books containing rare plates have the plates foxed or otherwise damaged, and it is sometimes possible, in rebinding such books, to substitute for the injured plates other perfect ones, in exact facsimile, from some later edition of the same book. Suspicion of this, or of other tampering, can generally be avoided when such books appear still in the original binding.

There is, moreover, a sentimental attraction in early issues of books in their original state, since, in most cases, they thus appear as they formerly did to their author, perhaps even in some special color or design of binding which he himself selected. Original bindings having a stamped design possess a more or less individual decoration, perhaps from the hand of some well-known artist. Aubrey Beardsley, for instance, prepared a number of such book decorations; many of the volumes issued in 1894-95 by John Lane of London, have cover designs by this artist and these, especially when accompanied by a Frontispiece of Title design by the same hand, are often equal in interest to the text of the book itself. Of special interest from the standpoint of originality are the Japanese-like fabrics used in binding some of the first editions of books by Lafcadio Hearn. Whether specially decorated or not, however, the original binding is part of the individuality of a book and cannot be removed without destroying a certain part of its interest.

In the case of valuable books which are, for one reason or another, seldom referred to, or unique or presentation copies, it is a good practice to make slight essential repairs without disturbing the binding and to order, from an experienced binder, a book-shaped slip-case in which the volume may be preserved in its original covers without being subject to further wear or to injury from dust.

A fairly valuable book which must be rebound, should never be bound in calf or sheep, as these leathers, even when of the best quality, are very perishable. Sheep bindings, sometimes three hundred years old, may still be occasionally met with in remarkably solid condition. But the secret of such leather tanning seems to have been lost, and the modern sheep or calf binding cannot be counted on, even under the most favorable conditions, for more than one-tenth that length of time. In certain climates, parchment or vellum makes a durable binding which, with age, acquires a beautiful, ivory-like surface tone; but these skins will warp the boards unless the book is kept closely set in on the shelf. Turkey morocco is durable when well tanned, as it usually is. The best leather, for appearance and endurance, and also the most expensive, is red levant morocco. For efficiency and richness, although this is a matter on which tastes vary, it is best left "uncrushed" or, at least, only lightly pressed.

The best moroccos are those tanned entirely "acid-free," or as nearly so as possible. "Niger" morocco, native tanned on the banks of the Niger River in Africa, and imported into England, is an acid-free leather used for expensive bindings. This leather is rather hard to secure, but its desirability is indicated by the fact that it is the only leather on which the severe tests described in the Report of the Committee on Leather for Bookbindings, elsewhere mentioned, had no effect.

CHAPTER VI
THE BOOK SHELVES

LEATHER SLIP-COVERS

Open shelves undoubtedly form the ideal resting place for books, since they are not only convenient for access, but also allow a free circulation of air around the volumes. They are, however, often impracticable as affording insufficient protection against dust and dirt, especially in cities, where closed cases are very necessary. No case with movable doors is absolutely dust-proof, but some types very closely approach this desirable state.

Closed cases are, of course, to be preferred with glass doors to reveal a glimpse of the treasures within. They should be set a few inches away from the wall, to permit a free circulation of air around them, and should never be so placed that the books are exposed to direct sunlight or a strong glare, as this will fade or discolor the bindings, particularly green leather, which is very apt to turn brown. The room in which cases are placed should be free from damp, and the windows should be kept closed at night. If the windows admit an excess of sunlight or glare, they are best furnished with yellowish or olive-green glass, which will neutralize any harmful effects of the light on the books. Such colored glass, if "leaded," may be made a very attractive addition to the appearance of the room. Red glass verging toward the orange is equally effective, but less adaptable to the purpose.

A full description of the effects of light on various kinds and colors of leathers will be found in the Report of the Committee on Leather for Bookbindings, London, Bell, 1905. This report also gives the following suggestion for a preservative finish to be used on leather bindings: "Boil eight parts of stearic acid and one part of caustic soda in fifty parts of water, until dissolved. Then add one hundred and fifty parts of cold water and stir until the substance sets into a jelly. Apply this jelly thinly with a sponge or rag and, when it has dried, polish the leather with a soft flannel. If a white film rises to the surface of the leather this can be wiped away with a damp cloth and the leather repolished." A fair supply of this mixture, suitable for small library purposes, can be made by boiling half an ounce (by weight) of the stearic acid, and one-sixteenth of an ounce (by weight) of the caustic soda, in three liquid ounces of water and then adding nine liquid ounces of cold water. It is best to stir the mixture gently while cooling; the entire process of preparation will take only a few minutes. If kept for more than a week or two, this mixture may become mouldy. It is better to prepare it only when it can be used on a number of books at once.

Books in closed cases should be removed and thoroughly dusted at least once a year, the tops especially being carefully wiped clean, if gilt, or brushed, if uncut, in either case while holding the book tightly closed. They should be aired at the same time, particularly those not in frequent use. For this airing and cleaning a warm, sunny day should be selected and, whenever possible, on such days the cases should be opened; books, like people, are healthier when well supplied with good, fresh air.

Books on the shelves should set in firmly among their neighbors, as a certain amount of pressure on the sides is essential to keep the boards from warping. Care must be taken, however, not to wedge them in too tightly; such a cure is worse in its effects than the disease. The usual method of removing a book from the shelf is to hook a finger into the top of the back, or head-cap, and pull. Paper or cloth backs are often torn at the top in this way. It is far preferable to reach in with the hand and push the book out from the fore-edge or, at least, to tilt it outward by a slight pressure of several fingers on the top beyond the head-band. If the shelves are lined with velvet, as elsewhere suggested, it will be necessary to lift the heavier books into place when returning them to the shelves; if they are shoved in on the lower edges of the boards the velvet will follow them in.

Books in delicate bindings or fragile covers may often, with advantage, be fitted with slip-covers of silk, cloth, Japan vellum, or even soft, heavy paper. These covers are simple and easy to make, but they can be used only when the condition of the book will permit both boards

Fig. A

to bend backward without injury, while slipping the cover on or off. (Fig. A.) Covers of this kind, made of leather and provided with a label on the back, are especially adaptable to paper-covered books which, for any reason, one may wish to preserve in their original wrappers without rebinding.

Book-worms are practically unknown in America, but should active traces of these be found in a book the volume should be isolated at once and placed in a tight box with cotton well moistened with ether. Several treatments of this kind, at intervals of two or three days, will kill any worms or eggs. Snuff or tobacco, to be renewed at intervals, placed along the back of the shelves, is said to discourage worms or other insects. Worm holes in old books may sometimes be filled in, if one has time for the operation, with a paste obtained by boiling down shreds of paper in sizing. The writer has an edition of Homer printed at Basel in 1535, in which a worm hole varying in size from one-eighth inch in diameter downwards, and extending through nearly one hundred sheets, has been filled in so carefully on each sheet, in this way, that the repair is noticeable only on the closest inspection.

Moths should never be allowed to breed in the cases. Were it not for increasing this danger the shelf lining mentioned above could be made of felt instead of velvet, the former being, otherwise, a more satisfactory material for the purpose.

While it is only in extremely large collections, where books are left undisturbed for years, that worms, moths, dust, and other enemies of books obtain enough of a foothold to do any serious damage, the careful supervision of even a small collection may sometimes prove of unexpected preventive value and, in any case, the slight extra trouble involved is in no sense a wasted effort.

The collector will also find it convenient to catalogue the books in his cases, preferably by means of a card-index system. Cards three by five inches usually will be found large enough to hold a fair description. Each card should be headed with the author's name, for convenience in indexing, followed by the book title, an exact transcript of the title-page or colophon, a description of the illustrations, if any, the size and the binding, and any bibliographical notes of interest. The price paid for the book, written in cipher, and the date purchased, should also be added.

The matter of correctly noting the size of books for such a catalogue or index is one to which the amateur will be obliged to give a certain amount of study, and he will find, among bookmen, wide differences of opinion as to the proper methods to follow. For all ordinary purposes, the descriptions of folio, where the sheets are folded into two; quarto (4to), where the sheets are folded into four; eight sizes of octavo (8vo), from fcap. to imperial, where the sheets are folded into eight; duodecimo (12mo); and sextodecimo (16mo) will be found sufficient. Speaking generally, a 4to will have a page signature at the foot of every fourth page, an 8vo at the foot of every eighth page, a 12mo at the foot of every fourth or twelfth page, etc. The old standard for octave sizes (measured on the edge of the pages, not the boards), which may safely be followed, is given in the table below. The sizes will be found to vary somewhat, where the book has been trimmed or where the paper used has been of an odd size.

Table of Octavo sheets, folded:

4¼" x 7"	fcap 8vo
5" x 7½"	crown 8vo
5½" x 7½"	post 8vo
5½" x 8"	demy 8vo
6" x 9½"	8vo
6½" x 10"	roy 8vo
8¼" x 11½"	imp 8vo

CHAPTER VII
BOOK BUYING

KELMSCOTT PRESS BOOK

As by far the greater portion of rare and desirable books to be had in America from time to time are sent over from England and the Continent by dealers' agents, it follows that the amateur collector in this country must depend largely on dealers for his supply of books. Except at auctions, there are comparatively few opportunities of buying at first-hand, although rare items of American printed books are sometimes unearthed and, in the old book stores of the larger cities, bargains are not uncommon. These latter, however, are usually limited, at best, to picking up some good first edition of a modern author, worth, perhaps, five dollars, and carelessly marked, with numbers of other books, at about twenty-five cents. Better fortune sometimes attends. For example, one may sometimes find a really rare and valuable book which, in dim but inadequate realization of its value, has been marked higher than its neighbors—perhaps up to about one-tenth of its real value. Such an incident, however, is among the exceptions.

In any case, the stories of wonderful finds in years past, along the quays of Paris or in the stalls of London are, for the American at least, almost like romances which could never come true.

In buying from dealers, especially those who specialize in rare books, it is often, unfortunately, necessary that the bibliophile of moderate means, to whom these pages are particularly addressed, is obliged to pause before the price of some much desired volume. His buying problems are much more complex than those of his wealthy fellow-collector, to whom price is little object, since he must not only hunt out the volumes he wants, but also copies priced reasonably to be within his reach. Blessed, indeed, is the willing self-denial which produces the ransom of a good book, at the expense of the ephemeral luxuries of life! But under such conditions it is essential that the amateur have a fairly complete knowledge of the value of books, particularly along his own special lines, in order that he may not be driven to unnecessary hardships through paying unjustly high prices for his treasures.

While the prices of books vary greatly, according to condition and binding, they also vary to an astonishing extent with various dealers. The prices marked by some dealers are often high for certain kinds of books and low for others. Bargains often may be secured from the dealer who marks his books, not according to their present market value, but according to the price he himself paid for them, since it follows, naturally, that a bargain for him is a bargain for his customer. Information of this kind, in respect to particular dealers, is very valuable to the amateur who visits their shops, but he often gains it only after considerable experience.

Cautious buying, so often sneered at, is, nevertheless, essential, and the amateur bibliophile owes to himself not only complete information as to the "right" editions of books, but also a thoroughly developed knowledge and judgment which will enable him to value books with fair accuracy. He must realize that in many cases the dealer is wily and seductive; moreover, his wares plead for themselves to trouble the heart of the hesitating purchaser. He also must develop a certain amount of guile, and must be able to harden his heart, if necessary, against all appeal. This is one of the most difficult of all things to do, and is the triumph of knowledge over ingenuousness and of reason over bibliomania.

To the collector of moderate means, even though his library be small, his books represent a certain form of investment, fairly secured. It has been pointed out by Mr. J. H. Slater, editor of the English "Book Prices Current," that books bought as an investment are not really so, because to be a good investment they would have constantly to increase in value to equal the income from the purchase price, had it been invested in another way. This increase in value, however, often actually takes place, and in a fair sized collection of books, judiciously gathered, the abnormal increase in the value of some volumes will help to balance the sluggishness or depreciation of others. The bibliophile, however, may well rest content, and consider himself well repaid for his efforts to buy carefully, if the value of his collection as a whole remains equal to the sum total of his expenditures, and he may accept the pleasures of possessing and reading the volumes in lieu of interest on the investment.

To get a general idea of the run of prices, the collector should obtain as many priced dealers' catalogues as possible and study these carefully, in making comparisons noticing any description of condition or binding which might account for a difference in price between two copies of the same work catalogued by different dealers. He should also study the volumes of "Book Prices Current," both the English and American editions, which are issued each year to subscribers and may be found at almost any large public library. These books, for each year, give the prices realized at auction during the year before, for all books which brought over three dollars. These prices, however, must be considered with caution, as they do not always represent true values, particularly in reference to sales in Great Britain, where the operation of dealer's "knockout" cliques, conspiring to keep prices low, except on items where collectors bid direct, has been the cause of much scandal.

Advance catalogues of books to be sold at auction will be mailed by the auction houses, on request. At auctions free from suspicion of unfairness, the amateur will often find it to his advantage to buy, since he generally has a certain amount of advantage over the dealer, not being obliged to buy books so low that he may sell again at a good profit. He need anticipate little difficulty in competition over books of moderate value, provided he has taken the trouble thoroughly to inform himself as to the correctness of the edition he proposes to buy and is able intelligently to collate, either before the sale or immediately afterward. With items of considerable importance, it is sometimes a better plan for several reasons, under present auction conditions, to place the bid in the hands of a well-known, reliable dealer who will bid in the book for a small commission on the price paid, and who will assume responsibility for the book being correct and perfect as represented in the catalogue.

Books handsomely and elaborately bound, especially when bearing the imprint of some famous binder, generally command prices at auction and from dealers, rather in excess of their true value. There is always a ready market for such books among wealthy collectors. A desired book with the pages in good condition, but in a shabby binding, can generally be bought, and then equally well bound by a competent binder, at a saving under the price of another copy already resplendent in crushed levant. On the other hand, a book in an elaborately jeweled binding of excessive value often sells at auction for less than the original cost of the binding. A book bound by such a celebrated binder as Roger Payne will hold its value while the binding remains solid, with little dependence on the contents of the book itself.

These remarks, however, as all remarks about auction prices must be, are only general, for the varying state of supply and demand is often met with in extremes in the auction room.

As the market value of books changes constantly, and depends not only on varying rarity, but also on demand, it is necessary that the collector have some idea as to what constitutes rarity, and the conditions governing demand. For this a considerable amount of study is necessary. It has been pointed out that rarity itself does not make for value, if there is no demand. An unique copy of a book is necessarily rare, but if no one wants it, it will not bring a price in proportion to its scarcity. This is a hard rule which one must apply, and a rule often unjust to the books themselves. Yet, while there are many books of great merit slowly disappearing from the world because of neglect, it is also true that the books most in demand and commanding the highest prices in first or early editions are, in the main, books of great intrinsic merit, well known and, for one reason or another, justly famous.

The bibliophile must judge for himself as best he may, what books indicate by their nature and celebrity a permanent value and what books command excessive prices for the moment simply because of inflated interest and demand. Conditions governing market value change in large, general movements, often affecting whole classes of books. As an example, one may note the comparatively high prices paid a century or more ago for early editions of the Greek and Latin classics, while treasures of early English literature sold for a few shillings; while at the present time these conditions are almost entirely reversed and some almost unique classic volume in extraordinary condition is required to create much of a sensation. It may be remarked here, however, that the early classics, the foundation of our present language, should have a permanent value, if such an attribute can be rightly assigned to any books at all, and it may be assumed that almost certainly the day will come when these early and important works will again be in great demand and will bring prices all the higher because of the scarcity which has accrued to them in the meantime through the loss, in one way or another, of many of the extant copies.

The greatest care is necessary in purchasing modern editions, especially of modern authors, as the number of modern books and editions, whether the books be good, bad or indifferent—the latter two adjectives usually applying, unfortunately—present an extremely complex field from which only great foresight will select books of merit which will be sought after several generations hence.

The amateur should also observe with a certain amount of suspicion books printed in very "limited" editions, with a view of establishing immediate rarity, permitting himself an interest only in those of obvious merit, where the limited edition is not necessitated by limited demand, and avoiding those books so printed of which previous editions much in demand have been issued. Privately printed books in limited editions, such as the books issued by the Villon Society, which include John Payne's important translations from the French and Italian, and the various issues of the Kama Shastra Society (*), in which Sir Richard Burton, the gifted orientalist, was actively interested, being not only first editions and of marked literary merit, but also books fairly certain to be in demand, and rare, may generally be considered of sound value and interest. Books from famous private presses, examples of the highest state of typography of their time,

(*) This Society has been credited—or otherwise—with so many volumes, chiefly of an erotic nature, which it never issued, that a list of the genuine volumes, issued with the authority and consent of Sir Richard Burton, may be of interest. These are: Kama Sutra, of Vatsyayana, 1883; Amanga Ranga, of Kalyana Mall, 1885; The Beharistan, of Jami, 1887; The Gulistan, of Sa'di, 1888; Alf Laylah wa Laylah (The Book of the Thousand Nights and a Night), ten volumes, 1885; Supplemental Nights to The Book of the Thousand Nights and a Night, six volumes, 1886-1888. These volumes are all listed in a four page folder, which accompanied Vol. 5, of the Supplemental Nights. The

such as the Kelmscott Press books printed by William Morris, or books printed by some famous printer, such as John Baskerville, of Birmingham, are almost certain to increase substantially in value in the long run over their present-day prices and are, moreover, delightful books to have.

To be properly considered with the general subject of buying, are the special copies of volumes known as "association books." These are unique copies, connected in some direct way with the author or with some prominent personage. Because of the sentimental interest attached, these usually command high prices. Included under this heading are presentation copies with inscriptions by the author, the author's own copy of his book, generally with autograph corrections, and books with autograph annotations by some contemporary or later, but equally famous, person or author. There is no standard by which to judge the proper value of such special copies as they are unique, and such copies may change hands several times at close intervals

---

folder mentions two other volumes in preparation; The Nigaristan of Jawini, and The Scented Garden, of the Shaykh al-Nafzawi. The former translation was never issued; the latter translation, made by Sir Richard himself, was burned in MS by his wife, shortly after his death. The only translation of al-Nafzawi bearing the Kama Shastra Society imprint, was issued in 1886, in white vellum, uniform with the other single volumes listed above with the title of The Perfumed Garden. This translation, which was made through a French version, is described, and practically acknowledged as a book of the Society, in a foot-note on page 133, Vol. 10, of the Nights.

with a considerably varying but generally increasing price. Copies of this kind are generally held at high ransom by dealers, especially in the "high rent districts" of our large cities, and the amateur bibliophile is wiser to hope merely that, as sometimes happens, chance may throw such copies, until that time unrecognized as such, into his hands without extra premium. Dealers, and even collectors, often attempt to establish an association value in a book by inserting autograph letters or signatures of the author; but such volumes, although thus made of considerable interest, obviously cannot properly be considered under this heading.

CHAPTER VIII
THE GREEK AND LATIN CLASSICS

BLACK LETTER VIRGIL

The collections of first and early editions of the Greek and Latin classics in the original which, a century or two ago, formed the backbone of nearly all collections of note, have since, as mentioned elsewhere, lost much of their interest for the bibliophile. A rare, uncut editio princeps of Homer may still produce from its sale, as in Dibdin's day, "a little annuity," and perhaps an annuity which would have made Dibdin gasp; but this volume may possibly be considered an exception.

The present practical neglect of the Greek and Latin languages, except as college exercises, may in a certain measure be responsible for the modern lack of interest in the original classics, since the bibliophile may be pardoned, in a sense, for not buying books in which his interest is limited to possession and which he is unable to read with any degree of satisfaction.

The past three hundred years of English literature, however, have produced a great number of translations from these classics, the best, no doubt, being made by men of independent income with the ability and leisure to turn their hands toward such work. A careful sifting of these translations, therefore, might very well furnish the bibliophile who is inclined toward such reading with a library of classics easily readable in good, accurate translation. The cost of such a collection would be comparatively moderate, and if care were taken in the selection to obtain first or early editions of the translations recognized as having the best literary qualities, there is little reason to doubt that the collection would have a very positive value. The subject is, perhaps, interesting enough to justify a few details.

The principal stumbling block, and that which renders the ordinary published "classic" libraries of doubtful value, is the delicate question of expurgation and that of abridgment. Any translation is, at best, a substitute; but an incomplete one is worse than none at all. There are, however, a few volumes in which the collector will be interested, which will be obtained, in all their original naïvete, only with difficulty.

Suppose a nucleus for such a collection were to be assembled. One would, of course, begin with Homer. The best translation in prose is by Andrew Lang and others; the Iliad, 1883; the Odyssey, 1879. The most readable verse translation is that by William Cullen Bryant, in four volumes, Boston, 1870-1871. This version, unfortunately, gives the Roman form of the names of the Greek gods—a concession to unnecessary corruption—but is otherwise very faithful.

After Homer, perhaps Plato's Dialogues, of which the best translation is that by B. Jowett, in five volumes, Oxford, 1875, third edition, revised, 1892. And of Plutarch's Lives, which follows naturally, the translation called Dryden's, revised by Clough, five volumes, Boston and London, 1859. Virgil, from the Latins, would accompany these, and of this, a good translation is Dryden's also, revised this time by John Carey, in three volumes, London, 1803. A much rarer edition is the "Aeneidos" of Thomas Phaer, London, 1584, with several reprints, in small black letter.

As a souvenir of lovely Sicily, we would require, of course, the pastorals of Theocritus, of which the best translation is that in prose by Andrew Lang, London, 1880. In this rendering two passages of about two lines each are left untranslated, but the omission is too slight to be serious. The same volume also contains the poems of Bion and Moschus. A good verse translation is that by C. S. Calverley, Cambridge (England), 1869. With Theocritus we must read Sappho, "the poetess," the ancients called her, as they called Homer "the poet." Meleager, in the poem of his "Garland" of verse, says that he includes "of Sappho's only a few but all roses." And so, indeed, are the few precious fragments which have come down to us. All the known fragments of this poetess, even mere references or quotations of a word or a phrase from ancient writers, which have survived, have been gathered by H. T. Wharton, who gives in his little volume called Sappho, the Greek text and a literal translation of each fragment, together with various verse translations of interest. The first edition of this book appeared in 1885, the third and definite edition in 1895. Both were published in London; the former by David Stott, the latter by John Lane.

Of Anacreon's lyrics, only a few fragments remain. The Anacreontea were tranlsated by Thomas Stanley, London, 1651; reprinted by Lawrence and Bullen, London, 1893. The reprint may be had on Japan vellum and on vellum.

Of the Greek Anthology, the famous collection of Greek epigrams composed between about B. C. 450 and A. D. 550, there are many volumes of translated "selections." The best and most poetic, although the rendering is in prose, is that by J. W. Mackail, London, 1890, revised 1906 and 1911. The greater part of the Anthology, which contains over three thousand five hundred epigrams, was translated into readable verse by Major Robert McGregor, London, 1864, but the spirit of this rendering is indifferent. A complete translation into prose of the entire Anthology, omitting only the ultra-erotic and paederastic epigrams, is now in process of publication in five volumes by Heinemann, London. This would be, when complete, the most desirable all-around translation were it not for the bald and unpoetic literalness of the rendering; of which, as an instance, one could note the passage in the two hundred and twenty-fifth Amatory epigram, which might be translated, "I have a wound of love which never heals * * *"; but which is rendered, "My love is a running sore * * *"

With the poets, Catullus must be included; the best and only complete translation is that by Richard F. Burton and Leonard Smithers, London, privately printed, 1894. This volume gives the Latin text, a complete prose rendering by Smithers, and a characteristic verse rendering by Burton. In the latter, some erotic passages are missing, due, according to Lady Burton's statement, to an incomplete manuscript.

Among the dramatists there are Aeschylus, whose tragedies were translated in verse by R. Potter, London, 1777, and Sophocles, whose tragedies were translated by the same hand, London, 1788. Edward FitzGerald's rendering of the Agamemnon of Aeschylus, London, 1876, which does not, however, pretend to be a close translation, may well be included for the unusual beauty of its verse. The comedies of Terence have had several translators. The best close rendering is that in prose, privately printed by the "Roman Society," in two volumes, 1900-1901.

Copies of this translation are scarce, as the edition was limited to two hundred and sixty copies.

Aristophanes is, of course, essential, but of the eleven comedies of his which are extant, there is only one complete translation, that privately printed under the imprint of the "Athenian Society," in two volumes, London, 1912, and limited to six hundred and twenty-five copies. These comedies have, perhaps, no equal in all literature, except in Rabelais, and the translation mentioned not only does them full justice, although in prose, but also furnishes exhaustive and illuminating notes necessary for the full understanding of all the humor. Four of the comedies were translated into admirable verse by J. H. Frere, Malta, 1839, and are well worth having, although, of course, Aristophanes' frequent and characteristic "obscenities" are omitted.

Among the satirists we have the Latins, Martial and Juvenal, and the Greek Lucian. The best Martial in English is the "Ex Otio Negotium" of R. Fletcher, London, 1656, reprinted in an edition of one hundred and five copies in 1893. Only selected epigrams are given, those selected being rendered rather freely, but there is no semblance of emasculation and the essential genius of translation is present. A good Juvenal is the verse translation by Robert Stapylton, London, 1647. A fair prose rendering, with the Latin text, is found in an anonymous translation issued, with Sheridan's translation of Persius, in 1777. Of Lucian's many works, there are almost innumerable translations, nearly all of which are expurgated. A good rendering of Selected Dialogues is that by Howard Williams, London, Bell. The "True History," which contains, as might be expected, the wildest flights of imagination, was translated by Francis Hickes, London, 1634; privately reprinted in a limited edition, with the Greek text, in 1896.

The immortal "Golden Ass" of Lucius Apuleius is attractive in the quaint Elizabethan version of William Adlington, of which five editions in small black letter were printed between 1566 and 1639. A modern reprint was issued by David Nutt, London, in 1893. The translation is not always accurate, but it is sufficiently so and it is particularly treasured as a fine specimen of the prose of that period. Apuleius exists in complete translation in the rendering by F. D. Byrne, printed in Paris in 1904, in a limited and private edition. The edition has numerous indifferent plates, and was reprinted, in incomplete translation, with several plates omitted, under a London imprint, of the same date. The translation reads rather more easily than the rendering by Thomas Taylor, London, 1822, and includes the erotic passages which, like all similar passages in the classics, are incorporated with ingenuous shamelessness and are, as might be expected, quite harmless. For Taylor's translation, these "passages suppressed" were supplied on separate sheets.

Among the "impudiques et charmants," as Pierre Louys calls them, must be mentioned the famous Satyricon of Petronius, of which Charles Carrington has printed the only complete translation, with his own imprint, Paris 1902, in an edition of five hundred and fifteen copies, since reprinted. The first edition bears a slip attributing the translation to Oscar Wilde, but the work has not the slightest internal evidence to support this. Also the "Priapeia" a collection of Latin epigrams of the best period, all bearing on the god Priapus. Two hundred and fifty copies of a translation of this small anthology were issued by the Erotika Biblion Society, "Athens" 1888. Notes on various subjects occupy more than half the volume.

Of the early romances, the most desirable is doubtless the "Daphnis and Chloe" of Longus who wrote early in the Christian era. This work has been said to belong more to French than to Greek literature, so enthusiastically was it adopted in France; and, in fact, the first printed edition of the work, translated by Bishop Amyot in 1559, preceded the editio princeps of the Greek text by forty years. A great many French editions have been printed, some with charming illustrations. The edition with notes by A. Pons and vignettes by Scott, Paris, Quantin 1878, gives a full French translation of the

Greek text and an exhaustive bibliography in an attractive format. The only complete translation in English is that issued to subscribers by the Athenian Society in 1896.

This Athenian Society issued to two hundred and fifty legitimate subscribers, between the years 1895 and 1898, seven volumes of complete translations from the Greek, of which several volumes, like the Longus, were the first complete translations into English. On account of the very limited issue, the volumes are very scarce, especially in sets. The complete issue was as follows: Lucian: The Ass. Dialogues of Courtesans. Amores.—Procopius: Anecdota.—Alciphron: Letters.—Longus: Daphnis and Chloe.—Heliodorus; Three books of the Æthiopica.— Achilles Tatius: Four Books of The Loves of Cleitophon and Leucippe.—Aristophanes: The Acharnians. The Knights. The Clouds. The volumes also included the Greek text.

The general subject of classic translations is an interesting one and capable of almost infinite expansion. One might form a very imposing collection of books by merely gathering editions of Daphnis and Chloe, for instance. But the bibliophile, whether he collects Greek and Latin translations, or books on angling, can perhaps best follow his own taste and judgment, when once he has secured a nucleus from which to start, and fairly understands the possibilities—and limitations—of his subject.

These books—thin boards and sheets of fragile paper—have lived while countless men have died; through the rise and fall of princes; through wars and ruin and tempests.

Other hands, long since forgotten, have cared for them and kept them safely. Now they are here in trust with me; and I, in my turn, linger over them, hoping that other Owners, yet unborn, may treat them gently as I, and those before, have done.

INDEX

Association Books: 107
Auctions: 102
Autographs in books: 16, 25, 107
Autograph Letters in books: 108
Back, Lining up: 20, 48
Back, Shaken or broken: 19
Binding, Cheap: 78
       Elaborate: 103
       Original: 73, 83, 92
Bleaching: 33, 35
Book-worms: 93
Books as an investment: 101
Book sizes: 94
Catalogues: 102
Cataloguing: 94
Collating: 15
Corners, Repairing: 22, 63
Covers (leather), Cleaning: 51
                Patching: 55
                Polishing: 56, 90

Covers (leather), Restoring: 55
                    Transferring: 72
Dealers: 99
Dusting: 15, 91
Edges, Cleaning: 65
      Gilt or Uncut: 81
Finishing new back: 46
Gilt, Removing: 71
     Restoring: 67
Glaire: 59
Hinges, Repairing: 62
Ink, Brightening autographs in: 26
    Removing: 33, 54, 66
Inlaying covers: 60
Inlaying pages: 18
Inlays, Tinting: 18
Kama Shastra Society: 106
Leather for bindings: 39, 84
Leather Paste for inlays: 61
Light, Effect on books of: 90
Limited Editions: 106
Lining up backs: 20
Marginal MS Notes: 16
Margins, Trimming: 78
Modern Editions: 105
Niger Morocco: 85
Old Paper imitated: 18

Pages, Repairing torn: 17
Paste for repairs: 20
Presentation copies: 16, 84, 107
Preservative for leather: 40
Preservative Polish: 90
Privately Printed books: 106
Rarity of books: 104
Rebacking, Tools for: 47
Rebinding, Best leather for: 84
   Directions for: 80
   For Amateurs: 79
   Price of: 77, 82
   When advisable: 55
Report of the Committee on Leather for Bookbinding: 85, 90
Re-tinting: 31
Sewing: 82
Shelves, Lining for: 64, 91
Sizing: 22, 30
Slip-cases: 84
Slip-covers: 92
Spots, Small: 30, 54
Stains: 31
Stains of Blood: 34
   Egg Yellow: 33
   Fecal Matters or Urine: 34
   Fruit Juice: 34
   Grease: 31, 54

Stains of Ink: 33, 54, 66
        Mud: 33
        Sealing-wax or Resin: 32
        Stearine: 32
        Tar and Pitch: 32
        Unknown Origin: 30
        White or Yellow Wax: 32
Tools, Making: 68
Tooling: 46, 67
Tooling, Restoring old: 67
Transferred Impressions: 34
Varnish for bindings: 57
Vellum Bindings, Cleaning: 59
Velvet for shelves: 64, 91
Washing: 33, 35